WORKBOOK

For

WHITE FRAGILITY

Why it's So Hard for White People to Talk about Racism

ROBIN DIANGELO

Roger Press

ISBN: 978-1-952663-20-8

Table of Contents

ABOUT THE AUTHOR

ROBIN DIANGELO is an author and educator, working in the fields of critical discourse analysis and whiteness studies. As a true academician, she formerly tenured as a professor at the Westfield state University of multicultural education and also lectured at the University of Washington. There she twice earned herself the Student's Choice Award for the most outstanding Educator of the year, from the School of Social Work.

Diangelo's laudable feat didn't end there. For more than twenty years she has been a trainer and consultant on issues that bother on racial and social justice. She has a volume of publications and books in her name but the publication for which she is popular for is "White Fragility," – this spiked a national dialogue on race and has been cited on NPR, Color lines, the New York Times, the Atlantic, and Salon.

INTRODUCTION
We Can't Get There from Here

Racism is a strong word that has eaten deep into our society today. Racism simplified is the act of empowering the whites to have institutional and social power over the people of color.

White fragility is birthed from the feeling of entitlement, inequality, and superiority over the people of color. This menace eats very deep even in the face of weak racial stamina and racial discomfort (this is a very typical occurrence in North America today). Race has people feeling very uncomfortable (especially the whites); they feel it is morally unfair to be connected to the system of racism and feel greatly delicate when discussed.

Most whites are often on the defensive when been told that white has meaning. They exude so much intolerance to any form of racial stress and display emotions such as fear, anger, extreme silence, guilt, augmentation, and even withdrawal. White fragility is ignited by anxiety and discomfort which aims to reestablish white equilibrium by maintaining dominance in the racial pyramid. White fragility is not weak; it is an influential way to gain racial control and full protection that is advantageous to the white community even in the face of their intentional evasion of the subject of racism.

One would think that lack of diversity will make the whites long for this information as a result of the drought in the cross-racial interaction. The opposite is the case, they appear very displeased in racial workshops and do little or nothing to participate or contribute.

The bedrock of this anger and resistance displayed by the whites when race is discussed or when asked to listen to people of color is not far-fetched. In groups, here are some of the ways the whites feel about racism.

1. The whites living in suburban neighborhoods have no constant interaction with people of color are sure that they hold no racial animosity.
2. Racism is purely a case of bad people versus good people.
3. They are aware racism existed but that it ended in 1865 when slavery was believed to have ended.
4. They are uncomfortable with any form of suggestion that says being white comes with a special privilege, meaning, and advantage.
5. Some whites feel they are the oppressed group.

Though minute, there is such a thing as pillars of whiteness. They are those factors and beliefs that form our racial responses. They are;

1. The belief that bad people equals racist.

2. The belief that racism is a disconnected act done by individuals and not an intricately interconnected system.
3. The belief that whites are entitled and more deserving of a better life than people of color.

We have been taught to define racism in ways that can never be virtually understood by the whites. There is the presence of racial isolation and misinformation that blocks the true message of racism and its origin; thus making it unwelcoming and a rude shock to the system.

In our world today, a racist hates to be identified as one. Instead, they say they are racially progressive. All of these said goes to show the white fragility and its prominent effect on racism. The intention of this summary on *"White Fragility"* is to draw our attention to the aforementioned, prove its existence and how the whites consciously or unconsciously make life hard for people of color, especially the so-called white progressives. These acts keeps the people of color on their toes and strive to prove their worth daily by putting in so much energy in attaining things in life. The people of color work hard to improve themselves academically, relationship-wise, and forget what matters to them the most. Race affects every aspect of our lives and has a significant role to play in our future outcome. This is no attempt at solving racism but to turn the spotlight to a single aspect of white susceptibility, racial inequality, and how it feeds racism in the very ground that it stands: white fragility and what can be done to curb it.

CHAPTER 1

The Challenges of Talking to White People about Racism

The whites are taught not to see themselves in racial terms; they don't draw attention to their race or make a public show of how their race matters. They know race mattered but are comfortable with talking about theirs and not others.

The whites have strong but tacky opinions on racism. To be knowledgeable about a subject matter requires study in other to understand and interpret it accurately. Now, in this case, the white fragility inherent in the white community disrupts the racial historical knowledge from reaching the heart. They are fast to be defensive, quiet, argue, and any other form of drawbacks. This display is social forces set in place to hinder a successful or productive racial knowledge implantation so that the previous racial hierarchy is still in place. Examples of these forces are;

1. The belief of meritocracy and individualism.
2. Wrong representation of the people of color in the media.
3. Portraying whiteness as the ideal human being.
4. Separation in schools and their neighborhood.
5. Continuous disrupted history, taboos, warnings, and jokes about other races.

Racism is simply an intentional attempt at racial discrimination by corrupt individuals making the concerned divide feel that they are not part of the problem and have no need to learn race any further. The whites fail to understand the true display of socialization. This is so because they have grown to see themselves as unique and objective. It is wise that we comprehend the forces that drive our socialization. These include experiences and perceptions culled from our cultural lens.

Breaking down these two hindrances to racism in the western world; objectivity and individualism is a very tall order. Objectivity says that we can be free of all bias while individualism says that each of us is unique and we stand out from others (even those in our social groups). It is this belief system that makes it almost impossible for the whites to explore the collective parts of the white experience. Individualism births the feeling of entitlement that says everyone is unique only as it concerns our race, gender, and class; so not all opportunities are present in certain packages. The race is irrelevant to individualism and failure is not as a result of the present social structure but the individual.

Grouping as to what racism causes is practiced with or without us knowing. We want to be young and not old; we want to be rich and not poor. In our subconscious, we already start putting together strategies to remain in the group that brings us joy and comfort. The same applies to the subject matter; our minds are being shaped by what we see, hear and read in magazines, books, television, and practice traditionally, etc. We only get to understand ourselves better when in comparison with others; deserving and undeserving. Just like pretty and ugly having no meaning without the other so does the latter.

To understand race relations, one must first know how and why racial collectiveness matters. Nip racial identity grouping it the bud. The whites need to stop denying that they have a racial viewpoint which makes them biased; this only makes them difficult to change and examine. There is an urgent call for racial humility in the land and a restoration of peace and love. We can never comprehend new forms of racism without exploring and studying the patterns of group behavior and the effects they have on individuals.

Try to put aside your uniqueness hindering you from seeing the bigger picture of the society you live in, note; individualism will not take you there.

- **Lessons**
  1. Several white people fail to understand the process of socialization.
  2. Whites don't see themselves in racial terms.
  3. Whites have a wrong definition and opinion about racism.
  4. Racism is simply an intentional attempt at racial discrimination by corrupt individuals making the concerned divide feel that they are not part of the problem and have no need to learn about race.

5. We are all products of our culture; not separate from it.

- **Issues surrounding the subject matter**
  1. What is the real meaning of racism or who is a racist?

  _____
  _____
  _____
  _____
  _____
  _____

  2. How do you understand who you are by understanding who you aren't?

  _____
  _____
  _____
  _____
  _____

  3. How do the whites react to the racial viewpoint bias?

  _____
  _____
  _____
  _____
  _____
  _____
  _____

_____

_____

4. How do you intend to study the present forms of racism to help you comprehend racism?

_____

_____

_____

_____

_____

_____

- **Goals**
  1. Write down the steps you will take to enable you let go of the individual narrative of racism and embrace the collective information as a true member of an outstanding shared culture?

_____

_____

_____

_____

_____

_____

_____

_____

_____

_____

_____

_____

_____

- **Action steps**
    1. Purge your mind of all the errors and fallacious opinions you had of racism and know what it means and walk in this light.
- **Checklist**
    1. Drop off your individualism and objectivity before going to the next phase.

CHAPTER 2

Racism and White Supremacy

Over time we have come to believe that we all have individual biological and genetic traits that make us stand out racially. But know this, the idea of race as a biological hypothesis is not true; it is more socially constructed.

The physical characteristics we see are not the true definition of race as they are unreliable metrics of genetic variations. Also, race and its variations as it relates biologically are deep-rooted. To this end, it is wise that we understand the economic and social ventures that led science to bring together social and other resources alongside racial lines and why the organization in this case is enduring.

SOCIAL STRUCTURE OF RACE IN THE UNITED STATES

The United States was formed on Freedom and equality without regard to class and religion. Nevertheless, the US was also built on enslavement, abduction of the African race, the annihilation of the native people, and the seizure of the Mexican lands.

Thomas Jefferson a popular slave master discovered that there exist natural disparities between the races and asked that scientists find more information to validate that the black race was naturally inferior and culturally deficient. It is good to know that during this era, enslavements and colonization were largely justified due to the colossal economic gains. So we can say that race science was motivated by the selfish social and economic interests of the privileged masses known as whites. History had it that the scientists that embarked on this race research went with the notion that they already knew the answers to their search. Thus they asked questions like, "why are blacks inferior" and not "are blacks inferior"? In no less than a century, Jefferson's idea of racial disparity became the order of the day.

The worldly scientific general assumption of racial inferiority was so that unequal treatment was justified and that it is not what triggers unfair treatment. Ta-Nehisi Coates made a valid point when he says that racism began from exploiting the resources of the natives, followed by unequal races to defend this exploitation. Furthermore, a renowned historian in the person of Ibram Kendi explained in his National Book Award-winning work that those who benefitted from slavery, mass captivity, and segregation successfully created racist ideas of the people of color as being best deserving of captivity, slavery, and apartheid. Those on the advantageous end (those who this message is meant to please) are made to believe that something fundamental is wrong with the blacks and has nothing to do with slavery. And this is nothing but a systemic perception.

THE RACE PERCEPTION

As mentioned above, the idea of race was so that racial inequality is legitimized and that the white fraction is at an advantage all through. The white race was theorized more in the 1800s as more immigrants made their way into the US. Later in 1865 when slavery was abolished in the United States, racism continued in different forms till this very day. Even in this era, the people of color still struggle to have citizenship in the United States. As long as the court cannot scientifically and legally prove you are white, then you aren't. So the struggle started to be proven and accepted. Being white is based on the common understanding of the white man, so the court said. Once an immigrant learns English and gets acclimatize to the American customs and culture, then they become full Americans. Only European immigrants weren't exempted from being acclimatized and accepted as pure white and then, later on, other nationalities from across the globe were added to the sphere. So, we can say that race is a social structure, meaning that one can become a member of a race by understanding their language, speaking it, acting like them, and eating their foods. As long as you look and act like them, then you become one of them. The race is a result of social forces as seen along class lines; poor and working-class are not seen as completely white. Amongst the whites there exists classism between the poor and the working-class.

RACISM

Racism is not the same as discrimination and prejudice (prejudgment). It is important to know this to help you understand white fragility. Saying that whites have racial prejudice is the same as saying people of color are bad and should feel guilty as a result. As a result, we are left defending our character instead of exploring the foreseeable racial biases and find ways to alter them. This misconception is what hinders us from getting it right.

The American women's struggle for suffrage is a typical analogy of how formal power changes discrimination and prejudice into pillars of oppression. As seen that the men controlled the entire institutions, so the women were denied their rights. This is a similar case in racism, sexism, and any other form of oppression where a racial group practices prejudice backed by legal authority and influential control. This becomes the order of the day as racism becomes a huge part of the system. Another example is when the Women of color were denied the right to vote until the Voting Rights Acts of 1964. Racism starts from an idea, and then it spreads deep into society and becomes a norm.

Many whites don't acknowledge that racism still exists in our present-day; they see racism as a past event. Still, racial inequality is glary in the society between the whites and people of color as the whites turn a blind eye to it all the time. These racial disparity and segregation have been documented by some bodies such as the United Nations, US Census Bureau, and academic groups such as the UCLA Civil Rights

Project, NAACP, and the Anti-Defamation League. The truth about history will not go down the drain even if the White Supremacy refuses to accept or do something about the growing racism in the land.

The white privileges sum up what one stands to gain for being white. This the people of color cannot enjoy even though the whites have challenge but they have a laid down system that works.

WHITENESS AS A POSITION OF STATUS

Being white has a social and institutional glory backed by legal, economic, political, and social rights privileges accorded that quietly says —these privileges are only ours and none other. Today, being white has moved from mere privilege to a bestowed interest (legal entitlements), freedom of movement, mental liberty from the yoke of race, visibility, self-worth, positive expectations, sense of belonging and above all a sense of entitlement.

Writers of color, James Baldwin and W. E. B. Du Bois have written about whiteness for over many decades. These writers pointed out that the whites have refused to pay attention to what it means to be white in our society that is significantly divided by race. They admit there is no "Negro Problem" but a "white problem" yet there is still celebration of Black History Month, Civil War, and Civil Rights eras which all occurred in conjunction with the US history. Simply put, there is no US history without the struggle of freedom from slavery for the people of color – if not their history is based on lies. But; in the celebration of memorable Black days, it would be a lot better if we celebrated these dates without reinforcing whiteness. Naming whiteness only suggests that it has a meaning and gives an unmerited advantage to those involved, thereby triggering the defensive responses of white fragility.

WHITE SUPREMACY

The image of white supremacy exceeds the black and white-colored photograph of what we watched on the TV. There are clips of whites beating up black people at lunch counters, bombing black churches and all... although it is a useful term to collate the broad centrality and rumored supremacy of the whites. White supremacy has to do with the economic, political, and social system of domination. Mills posited that white supremacy is rarely acknowledged and there is no way we can study a sociopolitical system void of addressing how it was reconciled by race. This goes to say that for a fact, white supremacy isn't visible but it is almost impossible to live without it because of all the benefits ascribed to being white.

This is also seen in the financial global statistics where Americans keep topping the charts as the most wealthy and most influential. It is same in the American political, military, media, educational and health sectors; filled with more than 90 percent of whites. The white nationalists detached themselves from racist terms and white supremacy just to gain greater charm in the society.

THE WHITE RACIAL FRAME

The white racial frame is deep and rests on white supremacy. This frame is composed of stories, images, interpretations, silences, omissions that are passed from generation to generation. It circulates openly and covertly based on the medium used to convey the message. This frame sees the whites as superior in accomplishments and culture; while the people of color are commonly seen as people of less economic, social, and political stature. It makes whites dominate almost all the spheres of the nation which is often taken for levity.

What messages do our children receive on racial socialization? What are their teachers teaching them about their history and the history of others? The schools have a big role to play in this treatise whether we like it or not. Are our kid's schools making them more or less white? Why do we live separately when you say we are equal? Why do we describe the white neighborhoods with such tranquil and safe descriptions and the exact opposite for the people of color? What is so shameful about having dark skin? Why is it that white children are thought from a tender age to circumvent discussions on race and turn a blind eye to racial inequality? What answers have you been able to come up with as regards the above questions? You will see how deep racial socialization has eaten.

- **Lessons**
    1. Race is more socially constructed.

2. The physical characteristics we see are not the true definition of race as they are unreliable metrics of genetic variation.
3. The United States was formed on Freedom and equality without regard to class and religion.
4. Racism is not the same as discrimination and prejudice.
5. Today, being white has moved from mere privilege to bestowed interest (legal entitlements), freedom of movement, and mental liberty from the yoke of race.
6. White supremacy is the economic, political, and social system of domination by the whites.

- **Issues surrounding the subject matter**
    1. How is racism a structure and not an event?

    _____

    _____

    _____

    _____

    _____

    _____

    2. Which side of the divide are you and why do you think you belong there and not on the other?

    _____

    _____

    _____

    _____

    _____

    _____

    _____

3. Tell the much you know about your native history (concisely)?

_____

_____

_____

_____

_____

_____

_____

_____

_____

_____

_____

4. Do you think racism can ever be eliminated from the world, if no – explain why, and if yes – explain how we should go about it?

_____

_____

_____

_____

_____

_____

- **Goals**
  1. In what ways will the black history be incorporated in school curriculums and other widely spread journals to let every American know that their history cannot be told without that of the people of color?

_____

_____

_____

_____

_____

_____

_____

_____

_____

_____

2. For white supremacy to be abolished and for all to live equal lives, what can be done to end this reign of terror?

_____

_____

_____

_____

_____

3. In actuality do you agree that the white race is the superior race in the universe and they deserve better than anyone else?

_____

_____

_____

_____

_____

- **Action steps**
  1. There is a need for a re-doctrine of black history and how we all can co-exist multi-dimensionally and peaceably.
  2. There is no need for protests and riots if inequality is nipped in the bud.
- **Checklist**
  1. Every human is superior; no sect, nation, or group is higher or more superior to the other.

CHAPTER 3

Racism after the Civil Rights Movement

After the Civil Rights Movement is "new racism". This is the adaptive and hidden form racism has taken overtime. Thus it slips into the system through modern norms, practices, and policies. Racism's adaptability makes it still exist till date. All systems of oppression adapt and adjust to challenges and still uphold inequality. Nevertheless, systems of oppression are flexible just the way the LGBTQI (lesbian, gay, bisexual, transgender, queer or questioning, and intersex) community had their way to getting their demands met. So, why is that of racism and inequality refuted?

COLOR-BLIND RACISM

Color-blind racism is when racism adapts to cultural changes. It is simple; we pretend not to notice racism and it becomes non-existent. Color-blind racism is the worst of its kind. The civil right practices was captured and shown on the TV for all to see as they meted out horror on the black race but no one did anything to stop or change it. Color blindness then became the cure for racism and pretended not to see race or that it had no meaning to them. It is clearer by now that the Civil rights movement didn't put an end to racism. Now the world is saying that only racists say that race matters; thus, only a racist acknowledges race.

The challenge of racism is that it is hugely unconscious, deeply rooted, and defensive when raised. This unspoken bias brings rise to aversive racism.

AVERSIVE RACISM

Aversive racism is the sort of racism that is manifested by those who see themselves as learned and progressives. The whites maintain an optimistic self-image while enacting racism and they blame the people of color for their fate. The term "race talk" has become casual as it is now the ideal presentation of the daily life of racial signs that has no meaning than placing African Americans in the lowest level of the racial hierarchy. Yes, the subject of race is not one the whites publicly talk about, but it is displayed in their very actions.

CULTURAL RACISM

Race has eaten deep into our various cultural settings. As early as preschool, white children cultivate a sense of white superiority. Ever heard of "catch them young"? This emphasizes the importance of the need to imbibe morals in children at a young age because they will grow up with it. At this very young age, they are told that it is more privileged to be white than be anything else.

Many even said that the election of Barrack Obama displays sheer post-racialism, but you and I know that isn't true. A candid illustration showing you how the young and naïve perceives the people of color was displayed in the "doll test" on YouTube. The question now is what level of racism is young people exposed to / participates in, also how come that if a person is good, he can never be racist?

Types of race-conscious behaviors displayed by whites:
1. Acting too nice for comfort.
2. Avoiding contact
3. Imitating black mannerism.
4. Being watchful not to use racial labels.
5. Speaking deceptively negative about people of color.
6. Random violence meted out to people of color especially where other people of color aren't present.

- **Lessons**
    1. White racial framing achieves the consistent goals of uplifting whites while belittling people of color.
    2. New racism is the adaptive and hidden form of racism that allows racism to sip into the system through modern norms, practices, and policies.
    3. Color-blind racism is when racism adapts to cultural changes.
- **Issues surrounding the subject matter**
    1. How is it possible that no one claims to be racist but racism still exists?

    _____

    _____

    _____

    _____

    _____

    _____

    2. How does Color-blind belief make it difficult for us to address these unconscious ideologies?

    _____

    _____

_____

_____

_____

_____

_____

_____

_____

_____

- **Goals**
  1. How do we correct the white culture of how they perceive the people of color before it affects our future generation?

  _____

  _____

  _____

  _____

  _____

  2. What roles can family and friends, government, religious organizations, and NGOs play to end cultural racism?

  _____

  _____

  _____

  _____

  _____

  _____

  _____

  _____

_____

_____

- **Action steps**
  1. Charity begins at home, start indoctrinating yourself on what is right about race. It is not true that racists are the ones that speak about race. Talk about ways to end this menace with small and large discussion groups without remorse.
  2. Make conscious efforts to check the level of racial information you take in.
- **Checklist**
  1. Good people can also be racist.

CHAPTER 4

How Does Race Shape the Lives of White People?

Understanding the underlying foundation of white fragility is important to know why the whites react to race the way they do. It entails knowing what it is to be white and how it shapes our experiences, perspectives, and responses.

There are several traits to being white such as;

1. BELONGING

Before a white is birthed; they are conceived into a world where they feel belong. This reflects in their health care (they receive better health care than the people of color and would have whites at the top chain of the health facility while the people of color will be at the bottom). So it is easy for the people of color to forecast whether they will survive their birth, based on the race at play.

The whites feel belong in every facet of their lives; it reeks in the white infused neighborhood, as you turn on the TV, read a novel, read a journal, drive past billboards, a gathering predominantly of whites and watch a hit movie. The whites experience discomfort when they feel their sense of belonging is threatened.

2. FREEDOM FROM THE BURDEN OF RACE

This is a big burden if you have ever been in this shoe. Liberty from the shackles of race is a huge autonomy. Race oozes at our place of work and there are two tents pitched (the whites and the people of color) that cannot be evaded. It is overwhelmingly cumbersome to deal with racial issues everywhere you turn your head. In the face of racism, we don't see this maltreatment as our responsibility and thus stay clear; forgetting that not making attempts to curb it is the same as perpetuating it. This is encouraged by racial relaxation.

3. FREEDOM OF MOVEMENT

As whites, you have freedom to go about without suspicious eyes trailing you to and fro, or people of other races talking behind your back as you walk past. Race gives people surety to move around and also makes them uneasy depending on the side of the divide they are on and the case presented to them.

4. JUST PEOPLE

For many years, the white race has been bestowed to be the standard for humanity. Our lives have been so shaped from a very young age that anything outside the white race is substandard, unacceptable, and unaccredited. In school, we were given specific literature such as Charles Dickens, Ernest Hemingway, Jane Austen, John Steinbeck, Fyodor Dostoevsky, William Shakespeare, and Mark Twain. These set of writers are seen as signifying the universal human experience, and we get to read them because their pieces communicate to us all. On the other hand, we go to Maya Angelou, James Baldwin, Toni Morrison, and the likes for writings on Black History.

Images are used to portray the perfect human being – A blond with blue eyes and rosy cheeks...

5. WHITE SOLIDARITY

White solidarity is racial bonding as described by Christine Sleeter. It is the unsaid agreement of the whites to protect their interests and guard their fellow whites against racial discomfort. This they do systematically as they lay boundaries to wade off racial anxiety; this act is what white supremacy feeds on.

6. THE GOOD OLD DAYS

The white system avails them the opportunity to feel nostalgic about the good old days. This is a result of the white privileges they enjoy which it is a trademark of white supremacy.

On the other hand, the people of color can't make such reference knowing how horrific their past is. Filled with slavery, mindless killings, rape, genocide, selling off of black children, lynching, bans on black jury service, bans on voting, putting the blacks in inferior schools, educational discrimination, biased laws and policies, racist media presentation, perverted historical accounts and many more. There are no good old days for the people of color, nothing to reminisce about than hurt, pain, and longing for better days ahead. So the sense of superiority never ends.

7. WHITE RACIAL INNOCENCE

The Whites position themselves as racially innocent by not been raised to see themselves in racial terms. People of color are seen as racially guilty. Racial innocence of the whites is intentional to water down all the ill-treatment they meted out to the people of color and get away with it. This innocence aim is to act defensive and in sheer denial of knowing what the Black history is all about. Even if you never heard of it, aren't there quantifiable resources of the subject matter peering in your faces daily? There is no denying the nonexistence of racism but it becomes irritable to know that some people are intentionally trying to bury the black history and we are not having it.

8. SEGREGATED LIVES

The United States is deeply rooted and shaped by racial segregation. The segregation affects all the sectors of the society; in the schools, place of worship, social gathering, place of work, and even in our neighborhood at large. Neighborhoods are classified as good and bad based on the influx of people of color inhabiting there. The segregation only strengthens the fact that our experiences and perspectives are only what matters.

Segregation plays a huge role in shaping our lives. It dictates the entire way your life will go and the result. It even kills any form of cross-racial relationship.

Patterns for the foundation of white fragility:

1. A penchant for racial segregation.
2. Not understanding what racism is.

3. Perceiving themselves as individuals and excluded from the powers of racial socialization.
4. Lacking understanding that our history goes everywhere with us and that it matters.
5. Presuming that everyone has or can go through what we experience daily.
6. Discharging what we don't comprehend.
7. Lack of genuine interest in the views of people of color.
8. Jumping over the difficult, personal work to achieve solutions.
9. Mixing up a disagreement with lack of understanding.
10. The need to uphold white harmony just to appear good.
11. Guilt that neutralizes action.
12. Being defensive about the connection to racism.
13. Focusing on intentions more than impact.

- **Lessons**
  1. Understanding white fragility entails knowing what it is to be white and how it shapes our experiences, perspectives, and responses.
  2. Some of the traits of being white are belonging, segregated lives, freedom from the burden of race, white racial innocence, freedom of movement, the good old days, white solidarity, etc.
- **Issues surrounding the subject matter**
  1. How has race shaped your life?

_____
_____
_____
_____
_____

2. Do you think the development of an Indigenous child is equal with that of a white child having in mind the concept of white supremacy?

_____
_____
_____
_____
_____

3. Has speaking about racism ever threatened your career development, and how did you go about it?

_____
_____
_____
_____
_____

4. What is your take on racism not being a white problem?

_____
_____
_____
_____

_____

_____

- **Goals**
  1. How do you tackle the foundation of white fragility taking a cue from the patterns highlighted above?

  _____

  _____

  _____

  _____

  _____

  _____

  _____

  _____

  _____

  _____

  _____

- **Action steps**
  1. Put feasible measures in place to manage white solidarity, the belonging thingy, and more.
- **Checklist**
  1. It is our sole responsibility to deal with how socialization reveals itself every day in our lives and how we respond when faced with challenges.

CHAPTER 5

The Good/Bad Binary

Before the civil rights movements, the whites were audible about their racial superiority claims but after the civil rights movement, it is now a mutually exclusive ball game to be seen as good or rendered bad. Recall that it used to be openly said before that any skin in black is bad, well this hasn't changed except that the way it is been conveyed has adapted. It also used to be that good people don't indulge in racism except for bad people.

The civil rights movements became successful by simplifying racism to an extreme act of prejudice. It has to be built on the intentional, hateful, conscious distaste of an individual because of their race. Discussing these dynamics and placing ourselves in the equation is the start to ending racism. The good and bad binary hindered the average whites from understanding or stopping racism. This limited view of what racism is and its characteristics is the crux of the matter. Most whites feel it is until there is a murder by a white on a black man that is racist. It doesn't have to be this magnitude, there are several other traits carried out that kills a man, even if it isn't physically. Thus there is nothing true about the good and bad binary.

The good and bad binary conceals the structural nature of racism and makes it hard to see or comprehend. It is at play every single day as we go through our daily routine.

The way to go is to make racism visible so it is easily identified and put on check collectively. Let's break the white solidarity by ending racial stereotypes. Regrettably, the only thing white fragility can protect is the problematic behavior they get defensive about when accused of practicing racism. It doesn't go to tell that they are open and void of problematic racial behavior. This has me wondering what the whites qualify as racism. They label people good and can never be racist, they claim not to see color and that they value diversity. All of these claims rest solely on the good/bad binary.

Some examples of color-blind claims:

1. My family taught me to treat everyone the same.
2. I do not see color.
3. Race has no meaning to me.
4. My parents were never racist, so I can't be racist.
5. Everybody struggles, but if you work hard you will be successful like us.
6. Mr. A happens to be black, but that isn't the reason I am about to tell you what I am about to tell you.
7. Centering on race divides us.
8. Children are more outspoken today.
9. I'm not racist; I'm from ...
10. I was picked on for being white or I grew up poor (so I don't enjoy any race privilege). Any many more...

Always ask yourself, how does my claim function in the story I am about to tell in this conversation? When you get it right, you will discover that you have been able to converse effectively taking race off the table and close the gap to future exploration. Always have it in mind that our racial claims have underlying factors (beliefs supporting our racial claims), those we can see, and those which aren't visible.

Many other whites prove not to be racist by having people of color as friends which is still in the good /bad binary. Racism will still be at play in your cross-racial friendship. For kids, even when the race isn't discussed explicitly, they can internalize the implicit/explicit messages gotten from their environment and form an opinion that they carry all through their lives.

We cannot help but take our racial histories everywhere we go. Focusing on race doesn't divide us as most whites posit, nor does talking about racism makes one racist. Whites say culture in place of "race", not speaking about this vital subject matter is said to help them maintain their sense of "self" as unique individuals, forgetting that their socialization is incomplete void of group experience.

- **Lessons**
    1. We cannot treat everyone the same even though we are taught to do so because humans are not objective and with different needs and relationships with us.
    2. Before now it used to be openly said that any skin in black is bad, well this hasn't changed except that the way it is been conveyed has adapted.
    3. The civil rights movements became successful by simplifying racism to an extreme act of prejudice.
    4. Racism is built on the intentional, hateful, conscious distaste of an individual because of their race.
- Issues surrounding the subject matter
    1. Why do you think the whites avoid talks on race?

_____

_____

_____

_____

_____

2. Do whites having friends of color prove them not to be racist?

    _____

    _____

    _____

    _____

    _____

- **Goals**
    1. Whether you are white or a person of the color, have you been challenged to look at your racism and how did you go about it?

        _____

        _____

        _____

        _____

    2. How do you intend to be an agent of change and interrupt racism anytime it raises its ugly head?

        _____

        _____

        _____

        _____

_____

_____

- **Action steps**
    1. Always ask yourself, how does my claim function in the story I am about to tell in this conversation.
- **Checklist**
    1. There is a problem of misinformation that circulates and causes our differential treatment to be biased.

CHAPTER 6

Anti-Blackness

Racism is every ounce of complex and it manifests differently for various groups of color. The start of putting a stop to individualism and color blindness which are ideologies of racism is for whites to end their perception of themselves as more unique than any other race on planet earth.

There is a need to discuss white people but as a group, although the act may disrupt our unracialized identities. For the whites to talk about racism it goes against their individualism.

Practicing racial generalization can harm the people of color in ways that deny the particular ways various groups undergo racism.

There are some race variations ascribed to group members;

1. How they have adapted to the prevailing culture.
2. How they have been symbolized.
3. How they are positioned relating to other people of color.
4. The role the group is assigned by the prevailing society.

There exist distinctive anti-black sentiments basic to white identity. First, it is wise to tackle the notion the whites feel about blacks being the ultimate racial group and correct the racial socialization responsible for white fragility. Every white has an anti-black feeling resting inside that was nurtured from a very tender age regardless of friendship. The feeling is not something whites can help; the sentiments arise while passing blacks on the street, stereotypical presentation of blacks in the media, warnings, and jokes between the whites.

These feelings that we think are minute needs to be examined so they don't escalate to bigger hate and violence.

Here is something the whites hate to hear, but it is the truth... the segregation and separation of the black race created the supposed superior white race; so you see; they both wouldn't exist without the other. Same way, the whites need blacks as it is essential in the creation of the white identity.

Affirmative action program was instituted after the slavery era and lasts till date. This program was created to stop the discrimination against hiring but it goes with a lot of misinformation. It is believed that people of color are given preferential treatment in job hiring over whites. This is so untrue. This program was made for qualified minority applicants to have equal employment opportunities as whites.

But somehow this program has been swept under the carpet and the people of color went back to struggling at the organizational leadership level.

The highest level of discrimination is between blacks and whites and the least is between Asians and Whites. The anti-black sentiment is perceived by how swift clips of brutality towards black children and adult is vindicated by the whites, that it must have been a well-deserving treatment/judgment. It is also seen as an opportunity to reiterate that Black Lives Matter; all lives matter – blue lives matter.

Anti-blackness is embedded in misinformation, myths, parodies, forecasts, and lies. It comes from a place of guilt for what you have done and still do. It relates to the torture of the black race from past till present. Also, it is deeply rooted in our inability or unwillingness to discover the effects of history in our present-day and lack of historical knowledge.

Lastly, blacks are not people of rage and violence; they are humans with drive, ambition, purpose, aspirations, and rightful demands for complete and equal citizenship. Our need to deny the perplexing appearances of anti-blackness that exist at the top makes us irrational, and that absurdity is at the core of white fragility and the pain it inflicts the people of color.

- **Lessons**
    1. Racism is every ounce of complex and it manifests differently for various groups of color.
    2. Practicing racial generalization can harm the people of color in ways that deny the particular ways various groups undergo racism.
    3. White racial socialization provokes various contradictory feelings toward African Americans such as, compassion, bitterness, superiority, hate, and guilt that breaks out immediately ignited but yet can't be openly acknowledged.
- **Issues surrounding the subject matter**
    1. What is your take on anti-blackness?

    _____
    _____
    _____

_____

_____

_____

2. Do only black lives matter or all lives matter and why?

_____

_____

_____

_____

_____

- **Goals**

  1. As an individual and in a position to make a change in your society, how can you make known the fact about blacks not being people of rage and violence and that they are humans with drive, ambition, purpose, aspirations who rightfully demand complete and equal citizenship?

  _____

  _____

  _____

  _____

  _____

  2. In what ways will you end the act of racial generalization that can harm the people of color in ways that deny the particular ways various groups undergo racism?

  _____

  _____

_____

_____

_____

_____

- **Action steps**
    1. End racial generalization.
    2. Stop stereotypical presentation of blacks in the media.
- **Checklist**
    1. The separation and segregation of the black race created the supposed superior white race; so you see they both wouldn't exist without the other.

CHAPTER 7

Racial Triggers for White People

Identifying the racial activators for white people is imperative to know why they often run into protective mode when faced with racial matters. Whites display strong emotional reactions when faced with meritocracy, color blindness, and individualism issues. They become racially uncomfortable and less tolerant of racial anxiety.

Here are some reasons why whites are defensive about the subject matter and a typical racist system:

1. There are societal taboos about speaking openly about race.
2. Only racist are bad while none racists are good (the good/bad binary).
3. Presence of fear and bitterness to people of color.
4. The misconception that we are objective individuals.
5. Being guilty of the myth that there is more happening than we can or will admit.
6. Heavy investment in the system that benefits us both and that we have been forcefully conditioned to see as fair.
7. Adopted superiority and sense of a right to rule.
8. A weighty cultural legacy of anti-black sentiment.

Many white individuals are limited in their knowledge of what racism is and what it entails. Thus a reorientation is needed for the whites to fully understand the workings of racism and how it affects the people of color. Today most multicultural courses don't address white privilege nor does it talk directly about racism. These days coded language is obtained to express what they mean. Words like; urban, culture, inner-city, mainstream and disadvantaged in place of words like; white, privilege, racism, over-advantaged, individualism, etc. These coded forms of speaking tell us that they have a lot more to hide and indirectly showcase racism. All of these are just white fragility been displayed to it full.

Anthropologist Pierre Bourdieu came up with a concept of habitus to help understand white fragility and the certainty of the response of whites to racially challenged standpoints. He said habitus is a person's frequent way of identifying, interpreting, and reacting to the social signals around him/her. His theory has three key aspects relevant to white fragility, habitus, field (the actual social setting), and capital (the social value of individuals in a chosen field). All of these aspects exist to supplement the other, regardless of hierarchy or class. This system is advisable for seamless racial socialization.

Racial stress is real and some of the interruptions that triggers it are:

1. A challenge to objectivity.
2. A challenge to white taboos on speaking openly about race.
3. A challenge to the racial comfort, racial expectation, and entitlement of the whites.
4. Challenge of the kind of expectation we would get from the people of color.

5. A challenge to white racial innocence, white solidarity, individualism, universalism, white authority, and meritocracy.

White fragility may be theorized as the reaction produced and reproduced by the preceding and recurrent social and material benefits of whiteness. When imbalance takes place, thereby interrupting that which is familiar and taken for levity, white fragility is invoked to restore the equilibrium and earnings the capital lost due to the challenge.

- **Lessons**
    1. Identifying racial activators for white people is vital to know why they are often defensive and protective with racial matters.
    2. Many white individuals are limited in their knowledge of what racism is and what it entails.
- **Issues surrounding the subject matter**
    1. In what ways have you been racially stressed and how did you overcome it? Also, mention the interruptions that triggered the stress.

_____
_____
_____
_____
_____
_____
_____
_____
_____
_____

_____

_____

2. Has coded language come to stay? If yes, share your experiences and your reactions.

    _____

    _____

    _____

    _____

    _____

    _____

- **Goals**

    1. What measures would you put in place as indicators to identify racial activators for white people to know why they are protective and defensive in matters concerning race?

        _____

        _____

        _____

        _____

        _____

        _____

        _____

        _____

        _____

        _____

    2. Based on Anthropologist Pierre Bourdieu's concept of habitus to aid the understanding of white

fragility. Put his key concepts into play and explain how this concept can reform racism in your world.

_____

_____

_____

_____

_____

_____

- **Action steps**
  1. White reorientation on race and how it affects the people of color.
- **Checklist**
  1. To wade off racial anxiety, we have to watch out for racial triggers.

CHAPTER 8

The Result: White Fragility

As we carry our histories along with us everywhere we go, so does white fragility. Whites hate to see themselves in a racial context, so they make it a prejudice and discrimination affair and make it look like they are the ones been treated unjustly.

Today many whites say that discrimination exists against the people of color and another little fraction is saying that they have experienced it first-hand. For children, their perception of race is imbibed at a tender age. As young as they are they begin to display a sense of white superiority and information on racial control codes. They grow up opposing racism and denying their racially based privileges. Imagine how many children growing up with thwarted and manipulated information about race just to be racially comfortable at the expense of the people of color.

Other chapters have highlighted the character of white fragility, why it is in existence and the usual defensive way the world has responded to it over time. These formed responses now sound as a shield of moral character to protect against racial attacks while acting as though they are unaware of the history of the people of color.

They engage the use of violence which goes to show how delicate and uninformed they are in addressing racially related issues. The whites display confusion, digression, repetition, self-correction in a racial climate as they are not ready to explore their understanding of racism even on a basic level. This act of reluctance is what fuels white power because for as long as we cannot determine the official narratives and that which is stifled; cultural domination is a tall order.

White fragility can pass as a method of bullying. The white's ability to be sturdy in racial position is limited but the people of color are powerful and strong as strength is drawn from the awareness of our history and institutional power and dominance.

- **Lessons**
    1. Racial reluctance keeps the whites starved of other racial knowledge which is lethal as they will have no other option than to ordain white perceptions as universal.
    2. White fragility is another form of bullying.
    3. White fragility is much more than defensiveness; it is the sociology of dominance.
- **Issues surrounding the subject matter**
    1. As White fragility's mode of protection is self-defense; are they the ones blamed, victimized, and attacked when confronted with the racial discussion?

    _____
    _____
    _____
    _____
    _____
    _____

    2. What level of reluctance have you recorded as regards racial discussion?

_____

_____

_____

_____

_____

_____

3. Have you ever given thought to the white's reactions on racism display and how did it turn out?

_____

_____

_____

_____

_____

_____

_____

_____

_____

_____

- **Goals**
  1. What measures will you implore to make the whites more aware of their racist display in a less violent manner?

_____

_____

_____

_____

_____

_____

- **Action steps**
    1. Make intentional moves to end white fragility and its traits.
- **Checklist**
    1. White fragility needs to be checked on all grounds.

CHAPTER 9

White Fragility in Action

White fragility manifests in our everyday endeavors – characterized by easy traits. It is displayed at our place of work, school, church, cafeteria, hospital, and even on the street.

A popular representation of white fragility is outrage (to protect oneself from being perceived as racist). Here are some reactions white people have when their assumptions are questioned:

FEELINGS	BEHAVIORS	RACIAL CLAIMS	ASSUMPTIONS
Insulted	Denying	I marched in my sixties	It is a personal prejudice
Accused	Crying	Class is the real oppression	I am void of racism
Singled out	Emotional withdrawing	I am familiar with people of color	Let me judge if racism just occurred
Angry	Physically leaving	You are judging me	I don't need to know any more of racism
Scared	Seeking absolution	You have no idea who I am	Racism is only intentional
Ashamed	Focusing on intentions	You just played the race card	I am white and can best challenge racism
Attacked	Avoiding	What I said is harmless	Racists are bad people

Guilty	Arguing	You just generalized...	Racism is a piece of cake
Judged		That's your opinion	I have friends of color and can't be racist
Silenced		You just misunderstood me	

PURPOSES OF WHITE FRAGILITY

1. Uphold white solidarity.
2. Conceal off self-reflection.
3. Belittle the authenticity of racism.
4. Hush the discussion.
5. Make white people look like the victims.
6. Seize the conversation.
7. Protect a partial worldview.
8. Kill any trace of the subject of race.
9. Guard white privilege.
10. Center on the messenger; not the message.

- **Lessons**
  1. White fragility is visibly displayed at our place of work, school, church, cafeteria, hospital, and even on the street.
  2. A popular representation of white fragility is "outrage".
- **Issues surrounding the subject matter**
  1. Recount all the racial assumptions you are aware of and tell if they are valid, based on your new-found knowledge on white fragility.

  _____

  _____

  _____

  _____

  _____

  _____

  _____

  _____

  _____

  _____

  _____

  _____

  _____

  _____

- **Goals**
  1. How can you help someone see his/her racism without offending them?

  _____

  _____

_____

_____

_____

_____

- **Action steps**
    1. White fragility can be ignored and muted if approached rationally.
- **Checklist**
    1. The purpose of fragility is frightening but conquerable.

CHAPTER 10

White Fragility and the Rules of Engagement

The popular concept of racism says that only bad people who hate people of color can be racist. This position is wrong but can pose a serious threat racially. With statements like this, one can almost perceive that an era of change is far behind.

The only way to give feedback without activating white fragility is;

- Not giving it at all.
- Even if you still decide to; do this in the most subtle and mild manner void of emotions.
- You have to gain their trust by assuring him/her you are not racist.
- The feedback has to be based on an issue-free relationship.
- Give it immediately. Waiting long can be misinterpreted.
- Dish out feedbacks privately to avoid bad social transgression.
- Be as indirect as possible. Being direct is seen as insensitive.
- Make the receiver comfortable in other to be receptive.
- Don't highlight racial privileges.
- Acknowledge that you are aware his/her intention is good.
- Never say their behavior had a racist impact or be misunderstood.

Feedback is key to repair what is left of our social racial perception. In doing this; take note of how, when, and where you give the feedback.

Guidelines to help build trust with those you communicate with;

1. Never judge them.
2. Never make assumptions.
3. Assume the best of them.
4. Say the truth.
5. Respect.

- **Lessons**
  1. White fragility penalizes the person giving feedback and responds with silence.
  2. Responding to white fragility requires careful presentation, voice tone, emotions, and chosen diction in other not to destroy the situation more than it already is.
- **Issues surrounding the subject matter**
  1. How does one correct the perception of a white supremacist with rigid positions on race?

_____
_____
_____
_____
_____
_____
_____
_____

_____

_____

_____

_____

2. Can white fragility and white solidarity be extinguished and how?

_____

_____

_____

_____

_____

_____

_____

- **Goals**
   1. As a beginner or expert at addressing people on race, how do you intend to tackle the message and not the messenger even in the most unpleasant and violent scenario?

_____

_____

_____

_____

_____

_____

_____

_____

_____

_____

_____

- **Action steps**
    1. Identify your racist patterns and work to change them.
- **Checklist**
    1. Racism being the norm rather than an aberration needs to be quenched.

CHAPTER 11

White Women's Tears

It may seem funny, but the whites also cry about racism. They share in the racial pain of people of color (or so to say) and the blacks either believe them because it is truly coming from a sincere place or they know it is a smokescreen.

White tears speak of all the ways the white fragility is exhibited through the laments of white people over how difficult racism is.

A way white tear is displayed;

1. White women shed tears in cross-racial settings.

Here the whites feel entitled to shed tears for racial mistreatment meted out to the people of color while the people of color are left frustrated by the tears. You might say white women shedding tears at racial injustice is a good start to ending racism, but it is not so because our emotions are formed by beliefs and bias, and culture. We go around with our culture at heart and the black women won't take a white woman crying over black maltreatment, when history has it that black men were tortured and killed due to "white women's distress". Trust me the tears will only make things worse and will spike historical terrorism.

Ways white men showcase their fragility through dominance and intimidation;

1. Always wanting to speak first and taking full control over the conversation.
2. Proud and dishonest nullification of racial inequality by playing the devil's advocate.

3. Rude and simplistic declarations to the answers to racism.
4. Withdrawal and silence.
5. Playing reverse racism by acting as the outraged victim.
6. Aggressive body language.
7. Explaining racism with pride about the people of color.

Tears driven by white guilt remains self-indulgent and guilt functions as an excuse for inaction. Nevertheless, at times; tears are welcomed, as it can bear witness to the pain felt for people of color. But you have to be wise about how and when you cry without making a show of it.

- **Lessons**
  1. Insensitivity to the history of people of color is a typical example of individualism, white centrality, and lack of racial humility.
  2. An altered version of racism by the whites is to make race be about white grief, white distress, and white victimization.
- **Issues surrounding the subject matter**
  1. What is your take on the popular saying "When a White lady cries, a black man gets hurt" and what scenarios have you experienced this first-hand or heard about?

_____
_____
_____
_____
_____
_____

_____

_____

_____

_____

_____

_____

2. In your own opinion, what do you think makes white women cry about racism?

_____

_____

_____

_____

_____

_____

- **Goals**
    1. How do you intend to examine your reactions toward other people's emotions and how they may reinscribe gender hierarchies and race?

    _____

    _____

    _____

    _____

    _____

    2. What measures do you have in place to make sure our racial socialization doesn't set us up to reprise racist behavior?

    _____

    _____

    _____

_____

_____

_____

- **Action steps**
    1. We need to continually ask "how" our racism exhibits and not just "if".
- **Checklist**
    1. The reality is that whites want to learn how racism works but don't have the nerve to see how it truly works.

CONCLUSION

Where Do We Go from Here?

Racial socialization is a lifelong process, we keep learning, growing, and improving on it every single day. Subsequent chapters have explained the assumptions, emotions, claims, and behaviors of white fragility. All of these can change if we can change our racial pattern because dominant paradigm ruins the whole process of racial reparation.

When the whites give feedback from a transformed paradigm, even in the midst of the inevitable but mindless racist patterns, we tend to get different feelings and behaviors such as; compassion, gratitude, excitement, motivation, humility, guilt, discomfort, engaging, apology, reflection, listening, etc.

In tackling racism, we need to intentionally engage our claims, feelings, and behaviors the right way. It requires openness, transparency, humility, and respect. Let's be thankful and appreciate sincere feedback when it comes. Tell how helpful the feedback was, resist being on the defensive, focus on the message and not the messenger, find ways to build your capacity to manage discomfort and bear sincere witness to the agony of racism, don't be afraid to display your vulnerability, be curious and humble to learn more about other race (read books, watch films, a source for information on the website), show the world that you practice what you preach, build solid relationships and trust, don't encourage privilege protection/comfort, and discourage internalized superiority.

Developing a positive white identity is a fable and highly impossible. But what is possible is being less white by being racially aware. Get better education about racism, and challenge racial arrogance.

CPSIA information can be obtained
at www.ICGtesting.com
Printed in the USA
BVHW040003250620
582284BV00015B/605